TABLE OF CONTENTS

TABLE OF CONTENTS

THE ULTIMATE NINJA FOODI 2-BASKET AIR FRYER COOKBOOK FOR BEGINNERS

Delicious Complete Meals Made Easy with DualZone Air Fryer Technology | Full Colour Edition

Betty J. Lawson

Manufactured in the United States of America
Interior and Cover Designer: Danielle Rees
Art Producer: Brooke White
Editor: Aaliyah Lyons
Production Editor: Sienna Adams
Production Manager: Sarah Johnson
Photography: Michael Smith

TABLE OF CONTENTS

INTRODUCTION

Two years ago, for my birthday, my amazing friend Jessica gave me an air fryer. I was beyond excited, but honestly, I had some serious doubts about whether I'd be able to figure it out. I'm not the most skilled cook—I've always stuck to simple meals—and I was worried that this new gadget might just sit on my counter gathering dust.

But when I finally decided to give it a go, I was amazed at how easy it was to use! Even as a beginner, I found that the air fryer made cooking so simple. The food came out crispy, delicious, and way healthier than anything I'd ever made before. I couldn't believe it! It felt like I had just unlocked a whole new world of cooking.

Since then, I've become totally obsessed. I've spent hours researching new recipes, trying out different dishes, and learning how to make the most out of this incredible appliance. The best part? I get to share my recipe adventures on social media and connect with other food lovers who are just as excited as I am. Who knew an air fryer would change the way I look at cooking?

DEDICATION

To Jessica, I just want to say a massive thank you for the air fryer and for everything you've done to inspire and support me. Your gift didn't just elevate my cooking skills; it reignited my love for being in the kitchen. You've always been there to encourage me, pushing me to try new things and not be afraid of stepping out of my comfort zone. Because of you, I've had so much fun cooking and hosting parties, sharing meals with friends, and creating lasting memories. I'm truly grateful for your kindness and for always believing in me.

CHAPTER 1: UNLOCKING THE POWER OF THE NINJA FOODI 2-BASKET AIR FRYER

WHAT MAKES THE NINJA FOODI 2-BASKET AIR FRYER UNIQUE?

DUAL-BASKET DESIGN FOR EFFICIENT COOKING

The Ninja Foodi 2-Basket Air Fryer's standout feature is its dual-basket design, which allows you to cook two separate dishes at the same time. This is a major time-saver, especially when preparing a full meal. You can cook a main dish in one basket, such as chicken or fish, and a side dish in the other, like roasted vegetables or fries. By reducing the need for multiple cooking steps, it speeds up meal prep, so you can serve up a complete meal more quickly, without compromising on taste or quality.

VERSATILE COOKING FUNCTIONS FOR EVERY MEAL

This air fryer is not just about frying; it's a true multi-tasker. With functions for air frying, roasting, baking, and even reheating, the Ninja Foodi 2-Basket Air Fryer is suitable for a wide range of dishes. Whether you're making crispy snacks, baking a cake, or roasting a chicken, it can handle it all with ease. Its versatility means

you don't need to pull out multiple appliances for different tasks. You can air fry your chips, bake your bread, and roast your vegetables all in one device, making it a fantastic all-in-one tool for busy cooks.

SMART FEATURES: MATCH COOK AND SMART FINISH

The Ninja Foodi 2-Basket Air Fryer also includes advanced technology to ensure perfect results with minimal effort. The Smart Finish feature is especially useful when you're cooking two different dishes that require different temperatures or cooking times. For example, you could air fry crispy chicken in one basket and bake a dessert in the other. The air fryer will automatically adjust and ensure both dishes are done at the same time, so you don't have to manually time them yourself.

On the flip side, the Match Cook function is perfect when you want to prepare identical dishes in both baskets. This feature ensures that both baskets cook evenly and simultaneously, so whether you're doubling a recipe or cooking for a crowd, you'll achieve the same great results in both baskets. This is particularly helpful for larger meals or when you're preparing multiple servings, ensuring consistency across the entire batch.

WHY THESE FEATURES MATTER

The combination of dual baskets, versatile functions, and smart technology makes the Ninja Foodi 2-Basket Air Fryer more than just a convenient cooking appliance. It's a practical solution for busy individuals and families who want to save time while still enjoying delicious, healthy meals. The ability to cook multiple dishes at once, coupled with the precision of Smart Finish and Match Cook, makes meal preparation simpler, faster, and more efficient. Whether you're a beginner or a seasoned cook, these features help you get the most out of your air fryer with minimal effort.

KEY BENEFITS OF THE NINJA FOODI 2-BASKET AIR FRYER

CUTS COOKING TIME WITH DUAL BASKETS

One of the biggest advantages of the Ninja Foodi 2-Basket Air Fryer is its ability to cook two separate dishes at the same time, cutting your cooking time in half. Whether you're preparing a main dish and a side or two different components of the same meal, having dual baskets allows you to cook everything simultaneously without the need to wait between steps. For example, you could air fry chicken in one basket while roasting potatoes in the other, so everything is ready to serve at the same time. This feature is particularly useful when you're hosting guests or trying to get dinner on the table quickly after a busy day. By eliminating the need for multiple cooking sessions, the Ninja Foodi not only saves time but also reduces the number of dishes you need to clean afterward.

HEALTHIER MEALS WITH LESS OIL, CRISPY RESULTS

The Ninja Foodi 2-Basket Air Fryer is designed to create crispy, delicious food with significantly less oil than traditional frying methods. Air frying uses hot air circulation to cook food, giving it that golden, crunchy texture we all love, but with far fewer calories and less fat. This makes it easier to enjoy your favourite fried foods—like crispy fries, chicken wings, and even doughnuts—without the guilt. The air fryer's ability to crisp food to perfection while using up to 75% less fat compared to deep frying means you can indulge in healthier meals, without sacrificing flavour or texture. For those watching their calorie intake or following specific dietary guidelines, this is a game-changer. You can enjoy your favourite crispy dishes in a much healthier way, all while preserving the taste and texture you crave.

EASY-TO-USE INTERFACE FOR BEGINNERS

Despite its advanced features, the Ninja Foodi 2-Basket Air Fryer is incredibly user-friendly, making it an ideal choice for beginners. Its straightforward interface allows anyone to get started without feeling overwhelmed. The clear digital display shows precise temperature controls, cooking functions, and timer settings, so you don't need to guess or struggle with complicated instructions. For those who are new to air frying, the simple design of the control panel means you can quickly set the time and temperature for any recipe. Plus, with preset cooking functions for various dishes like air fry, roast, bake, and reheat, you can easily select the right option for your food with just a few taps. This ease of use eliminates the intimidation factor often associated with high-tech kitchen gadgets, making the air fryer accessible for anyone, regardless of their cooking experience.

THE CONVENIENCE FACTOR

With its dual-basket feature, reduced oil usage, and simple interface, the Ninja Foodi 2-Basket Air Fryer offers unmatched convenience. The ability to prepare an entire meal in one appliance, from start to finish, means you can spend less time in the kitchen and more time enjoying your food. The ease of use and efficiency make it a great tool for busy families, students, or anyone

correct temperature from the start. To preheat, simply turn on the air fryer and select the air fry function. Set the temperature according to your recipe—typically, 350°F to 400°F is the standard range for most air frying tasks. The air fryer will usually preheat for about 3 to 5 minutes, and a signal will alert you once it has reached the desired temperature. Some models may have a preheat button that makes this process even easier. You don't need to worry about preheating for too long, as air fryers heat up faster than traditional ovens. Once preheated, you can begin placing your food in the baskets, making sure to spread it out evenly for the best results.

looking to simplify their cooking routine without compromising on quality. Whether you're meal prepping for the week or whipping up a quick weeknight dinner, the Ninja Foodi's key benefits work together to make cooking easier, faster, and healthier.

GETTING STARTED WITH YOUR NINJA FOODI 2-BASKET AIR FRYER

SETTING UP AND PREHEATING THE AIR FRYER

Before you dive into cooking, it's important to set up your Ninja Foodi 2-Basket Air Fryer correctly for optimal performance. First, place the air fryer on a flat, heat-resistant surface with enough space around it for air circulation. Ensure that the appliance is plugged into a socket and that the baskets are properly inserted. The dual baskets should slide in easily, and make sure they're securely locked in place before turning the air fryer on.

Once everything is in place, it's time to preheat the air fryer. Preheating is an essential step to ensure your food cooks evenly and at the

UNDERSTANDING BASKET PLACEMENT AND COOKING TIMES

The Ninja Foodi 2-Basket Air Fryer allows you to cook two different dishes simultaneously, but it's important to understand the proper placement and how cooking times may vary. Place each dish in one of the baskets, ensuring that the food is not overcrowded. This allows hot air to circulate evenly around the ingredients, promoting even cooking and crisping. If you're cooking foods with different cook times, the Smart Finish feature can automatically adjust to ensure both dishes are done at the same time, no matter the cooking method or temperature.

For those new to air frying, don't forget that cooking times in the air fryer may be faster than traditional methods. Always check the recommended cook times in your recipe, but keep an eye on the food towards the end of the cycle to avoid overcooking.

SIMPLE CLEANING TIPS FOR LONG-LASTING USE

Proper cleaning is essential for keeping your Ninja Foodi 2-Basket Air Fryer in top condition and ensuring it works effectively for years to come. Luckily, cleaning this appliance is relatively simple and straightforward. After each use, make sure to turn off and unplug the air fryer, and allow it to cool down before cleaning.

Start by removing the baskets and tray, which are usually dishwasher safe. If you prefer to hand wash, use warm soapy water and a non-abrasive sponge to clean them thoroughly. Avoid using harsh chemicals or abrasive pads that could damage the non-stick coating. Wipe down the interior of the air fryer with a soft cloth or sponge to remove any grease or food particles.

For stubborn residues, you can use a damp cloth with a bit of vinegar or a mild detergent to help loosen grease.

Regularly check the heating element for any buildup and wipe it down gently with a damp cloth. Be sure to dry all parts thoroughly before reassembling the air fryer. Regular cleaning not only helps prevent the buildup of oils and food remnants but also keeps the air fryer performing at its best, ensuring that each meal cooks evenly and remains as healthy as possible.

Air Fryer Cooking Chart

Beef

Item	Temp (°F)	Time (mins)	Item	Temp (°F)	Time (mins)
Beef Eye Round Roast (4 lbs.)	400 °F	45 to 55	Meatballs (1-inch)	370 °F	7
Burger Patty (4 oz.)	370 °F	16 to 20	Meatballs (3-inch)	380 °F	10
Filet Mignon (8 oz.)	400 °F	18	Ribeye, bone-in (1-inch, 8 oz)	400 °F	10 to 15
Flank Steak (1.5 lbs.)	400 °F	12	Sirloin steaks (1-inch, 12 oz)	400 °F	9 to 14
Flank Steak (2 lbs.)	400 °F	20 to 28			

Chicken

Item	Temp (°F)	Time (mins)	Item	Temp (°F)	Time (mins)
Breasts, bone in (1 ¼ lb.)	370 °F	25	Legs, bone-in (1 ¾ lb.)	380 °F	30
Breasts, boneless (4 oz)	380 °F	12	Thighs, boneless (1 ½ lb.)	380 °F	18 to 20
Drumsticks (2 ½ lb.)	370 °F	20	Wings (2 lb.)	400 °F	12
Game Hen (halved 2 lb.)	390 °F	20	Whole Chicken	360 °F	75
Thighs, bone-in (2 lb.)	380 °F	22	Tenders	360 °F	8 to 10

Pork & Lamb

Item	Temp (°F)	Time (mins)	Item	Temp (°F)	Time (mins)
Bacon (regular)	400 °F	5 to 7	Pork Tenderloin	370 °F	15
Bacon (thick cut)	400 °F	6 to 10	Sausages	380 °F	15
Pork Loin (2 lb.)	360 °F	55	Lamb Loin Chops (1-inch thick)	400 °F	8 to 12
Pork Chops, bone in (1-inch, 6.5 oz)	400 °F	12	Rack of Lamb (1.5 – 2 lb.)	380 °F	22

Fish & Seafood

Item	Temp (°F)	Time (mins)	Item	Temp (°F)	Time (mins)
Calamari (8 oz)	400 °F	4	Tuna Steak	400 °F	7 to 10
Fish Fillet (1-inch, 8 oz)	400 °F	10	Scallops	400 °F	5 to 7
Salmon, fillet (6 oz)	380 °F	12	Shrimp	400 °F	5
Swordfish steak	400 °F	10			

Air Fryer Cooking Chart

Vegetables					
INGREDIENT	AMOUNT	PREPARATION	OIL	TEMP	COOK TIME
Asparagus	2 bunches	Cut in half, trim stems	2 Tbsp	420°F	12-15 mins
Beets	1½ lbs	Peel, cut in ½-inch cubes	1Tbsp	390°F	28-30 mins
Bell peppers (for roasting)	4 peppers	Cut in quarters, remove seeds	1Tbsp	400°F	15-20 mins
Broccoli	1 large head	Cut in 1-2-inch florets	1Tbsp	400°F	15-20 mins
Brussels sprouts	1lb	Cut in half, remove stems	1Tbsp	425°F	15-20 mins
Carrots	1lb	Peel, cut in ¼-inch rounds	1 Tbsp	425°F	10-15 mins
Cauliflower	1 head	Cut in 1-2-inch florets	2 Tbsp	400°F	20-22 mins
Corn on the cob	7 ears	Whole ears, remove husks	1 Tbps	400°F	14-17 mins
Green beans	1 bag (12 oz)	Trim	1 Tbps	420°F	18-20 mins
Kale (for chips)	4 oz	Tear into pieces,remove stems	None	325°F	5-8 mins
Mushrooms	16 oz	Rinse, slice thinly	1 Tbps	390°F	25-30 mins
Potatoes, russet	1½ lbs	Cut in 1-inch wedges	1 Tbps	390°F	25-30 mins
Potatoes, russet	1lb	Hand-cut fries, soak 30 mins in cold water, then pat dry	½ -3 Tbps	400°F	25-28 mins
Potatoes, sweet	1lb	Hand-cut fries, soak 30 mins in cold water, then pat dry	1 Tbps	400°F	25-28 mins
Zucchini	1lb	Cut in eighths lengthwise, then cut in half	1 Tbps	400°F	15-20 mins

CHAPTER 2: APPETIZERS AND SNACKS RECIPES

FIERY CHEESE STICKS WITH CRISPY SWEET POTATO WEDGES

Prep time: 15 minutes | **Cook time:** 25 minutes | Serves 4

Fiery Cheese Sticks (Basket 1):

- 1 large egg, beaten
- ½ cup plain breadcrumbs
- ¼ cup finely ground peanuts
- 1 tablespoon chili powder
- ¼ teaspoon ground coriander
- ¼ teaspoon red pepper flakes
- ⅛ teaspoon cayenne pepper
- 8 mozzarella string cheese sticks
- Cooking spray
- Marinara sauce or ranch dressing for serving

Sweet Potato Wedges (Basket 2):

- 2 medium sweet potatoes, cut into wedges
- 1 tablespoon olive oil
- ½ teaspoon smoked paprika
- ½ teaspoon garlic powder
- ¼ teaspoon ground cumin
- Salt and pepper to taste

1. Preheat the Ninja Foodi air fryer to 375°F.
2. In a shallow bowl, beat the egg.
3. On a separate plate, combine breadcrumbs, ground peanuts, chili powder, coriander, red pepper flakes, and cayenne pepper.
4. Dip each cheese stick into the beaten egg, then roll in the breadcrumb mixture, ensuring complete coverage.
5. Place the coated cheese sticks on a parchment-lined baking sheet and freeze for 30 minutes.
6. Toss the sweet potato wedges in olive oil, smoked paprika, garlic powder, cumin, salt, and pepper. Ensure they are evenly coated.
7. Lightly spray Basket 1 with cooking spray and arrange the frozen cheese sticks in a single layer.
8. Place the seasoned sweet potato wedges in Basket 2.
9. Set Basket 1 (Cheese Sticks) to 375°F for 7-9 minutes, or until golden and the cheese is melted.
10. Set Basket 2 (Sweet Potato Wedges) to 375°F for 18-20 minutes, flipping halfway through.
11. Serve the cheese sticks hot with marinara sauce or ranch dressing. Pair with the crispy sweet potato wedges for a perfect, satisfying snack or meal.

ARTICHOKE SAMOSAS WITH CRISPY CHICKPEA POPPERS

Prep time: 5 minutes | Cook time: 10 minutes | Serves 6

Artichoke Samosas:

- ½ cup finely chopped marinated artichoke hearts, drained
- ¼ cup ricotta cheese
- 1 egg white
- 3 tablespoons shredded mozzarella cheese
- ½ teaspoon dried thyme
- 6 phyllo dough sheets, thawed
- 2 tablespoons unsalted butter, melted
- 1 cup mango chutney for serving
- Cooking spray

Crispy Chickpea Poppers:

- 1 (15-ounce) can chickpeas, drained and patted dry
- 2 tablespoons olive oil
- 1 teaspoon smoked paprika
- ½ teaspoon garlic powder
- ½ teaspoon ground cumin
- ¼ teaspoon salt
- ¼ teaspoon black pepper

1. Preheat both baskets of the air fryer to 400°F.
2. In a small bowl, mix ricotta cheese, egg white, artichoke hearts, mozzarella, and thyme until well combined.
3. Cover phyllo dough with a damp kitchen towel to prevent drying.
4. Place one phyllo sheet on a clean work surface and cut into thirds lengthwise.
5. At the base of each strip, place about 1½ teaspoons of filling.
6. Fold the bottom right corner to the left side to create a triangle. Continue folding triangularly along the strip.
7. Brush each triangle with melted butter to seal the edges.
8. In a bowl, toss drained and dried chickpeas with olive oil, smoked paprika, garlic powder, cumin, salt, and black pepper.
9. Lightly spray both air fryer baskets with cooking spray.
10. In the first basket, place the samosas ensuring they don't touch.
11. In the second basket, spread the seasoned chickpeas in a single layer.
12. Samosas: Cook for 4 minutes or until golden and crisp.
13. Chickpeas: Cook for 8-10 minutes, shaking the basket halfway through to ensure even crispiness.
14. Transfer both to serving plates.
15. Serve samosas hot with mango chutney.
16. Serve chickpea poppers as a crunchy side dish.

BROCCOLI AND CARROT BITES WITH CRISPY PARMESAN ZUCCHINI FRIES

Prep time: 15 minutes | **Cook time:12 minutes** |**Serves 20**

Broccoli and Carrot Bites:

- 1 (10-ounce) bag frozen broccoli florets
- ½ cup shredded sharp Cheddar cheese
- 2 tablespoons grated carrot
- ½ cup blanched almond flour

- 1 large egg, beaten
- ¼ teaspoon kosher salt
- ¼ teaspoon ground black pepper
- Cooking spray

Parmesan Zucchini Fries:

- 2 medium zucchinis
- ½ cup grated Parmesan cheese
- ¼ cup breadcrumbs
- ½ teaspoon garlic powder

- ¼ teaspoon dried oregano
- Salt and pepper to taste
- Cooking spray

1. Cook broccoli according to package instructions.
2. Allow broccoli to cool for 5 minutes.
3. Use a clean kitchen towel to squeeze out excess moisture from the broccoli.
4. In a large mixing bowl, combine broccoli, Cheddar cheese, grated carrot, almond flour, beaten egg, salt, and pepper.
5. Mix thoroughly until well combined.
6. Preheat both baskets of the air fryer to 320°F.
7. Using a 2-tablespoon scoop, form the broccoli mixture into 20 small balls.
8. For the zucchini fries, cut zucchinis into thin, french fry-like strips.
9. In a separate bowl, mix Parmesan, breadcrumbs, garlic powder, oregano, salt, and pepper.
10. Lightly coat zucchini strips in the Parmesan mixture.
11. Cut parchment paper to fit both air fryer baskets.
12. Lightly spray parchment papers with cooking spray.
13. In one basket, arrange the broccoli and carrot bites in a single layer.
14. In the other basket, spread the zucchini fries in a single layer.
15. Air fry both baskets for 12 minutes, carefully flipping the items halfway through cooking.
16. Bites and fries should be golden brown when done.
17. Serve warm.

SWEET AND SPICY BEEF JERKY WITH SPICY ROASTED ALMONDS

Prep time: 5 minutes | **Cook time:** **4 hours** | **Serves** 4

- Beef Jerky:
- 1 pound eye of round beef, fat trimmed
- ¼ cup low-sodium soy sauce
- 2 tablespoons Sriracha hot sauce
- ½ teaspoon freshly ground black pepper
- 2 tablespoons brown sugar or granulated erythritol
- Spicy Roasted Almonds:
- 1 cup raw almonds
- 1 tablespoon olive oil
- ½ teaspoon smoked paprika
- ¼ teaspoon cayenne pepper
- ¼ teaspoon garlic powder
- Salt to taste

1. Trim beef and slice into ¼-inch thick strips.
2. In a large resealable plastic bag, combine soy sauce, Sriracha, black pepper, and sugar.
3. Add beef strips to the marinade, seal, and shake to coat evenly.
4. Refrigerate for at least 2 hours, preferably overnight.
5. Remove beef from marinade and pat dry with paper towels.
6. Preheat both baskets of the air fryer to 180°F.
7. In one basket, arrange marinated beef strips in a single layer.
8. In a bowl, toss almonds with olive oil, smoked paprika, cayenne pepper, garlic powder, and salt.
9. Spread seasoned almonds in a single layer in the second basket.
10. Dehydrate both baskets for 4 hours:
11. For beef jerky: Cook until dark brown and chewy
12. For almonds: Roast until golden and crisp (approximately 2-3 hours)
13. Cool both items completely before storing.
14. Store beef jerky in an airtight container in a cool, dry place for up to 2 weeks.
15. Store roasted almonds in an airtight container for up to 2 weeks.

SPINACH AND FETA POCKETS WITH MEDITERRANEAN ROASTED CHICKPEAS

Prep time: 20 minutes | Cook time: 10 minutes | Serves 4

Spinach and Feta Pockets:

- 2 large eggs
- 1 (10-ounce) package frozen chopped spinach, thawed and squeezed dry
- 1 cup crumbled feta cheese
- 2 garlic cloves, minced
- ¼ teaspoon ground black pepper
- 1 (13.8-ounce) tube refrigerated pizza dough
- Cooking spray

Mediterranean Roasted Chickpeas:

- 1 (15-ounce) can chickpeas, drained and patted dry
- 2 tablespoons olive oil
- 1 teaspoon dried oregano
- ½ teaspoon ground cumin
- ½ teaspoon smoked paprika
- ¼ teaspoon salt
- ¼ teaspoon black pepper
- Zest of half a lemon

1. Preheat both baskets of the air fryer to 425°F.
2. In a large bowl, beat the eggs, reserving 1 tablespoon for egg wash.
3. Mix thawed spinach, feta cheese, minced garlic, and pepper with the beaten eggs.
4. On a lightly floured surface, roll out the pizza dough to a 12-inch square.
5. Cut the dough into four 6-inch squares.
6. Place about 1/3 cup of spinach mixture in the center of each square.
7. Fold the dough over to create triangles, pinching edges to seal.
8. Cut small slits on top of each pocket.
9. Brush the tops with the reserved egg wash.
10. In a bowl, toss drained and dried chickpeas with olive oil, oregano, cumin, smoked paprika, salt, pepper, and lemon zest.
11. Lightly spray one basket with cooking spray and line with parchment paper.
12. Place spinach and feta pockets in a single layer, ensuring they don't touch.
13. Lightly spray the tops of the pockets with cooking spray.
14. In the second basket, spread seasoned chickpeas in a single layer.
15. Spinach and Feta Pockets: Cook for 10 minutes, or until golden brown.
16. Chickpeas: Cook for 10 minutes, shaking the basket halfway through to ensure even roasting.
17. Transfer both to serving plates.
18. Serve pockets hot with roasted chickpeas on the side.

CRISPY CALAMARI RINGS WITH SEASONED SWEET POTATO FRIES

Prep time: 10 minutes | Cook time: 15 minutes | Serves 4

Crispy Calamari Rings (Basket 1):

- 1 pound calamari rings, patted dry
- 3 tablespoons fresh lemon juice
- ½ cup all-purpose flour
- 1 teaspoon garlic powder
- 2 egg whites
- ¼ cup whole milk
- 1½ cups panko breadcrumbs
- 1½ teaspoons kosher salt
- 1½ teaspoons ground black pepper
- Cooking spray

Seasoned Sweet Potato Fries (Basket 2):

- 2 medium sweet potatoes, peeled and cut into thin fries
- 1 tablespoon olive oil
- 1 teaspoon paprika
- ½ teaspoon garlic powder
- ½ teaspoon smoked paprika (optional)
- ½ teaspoon kosher salt
- ¼ teaspoon ground black pepper

1. In a medium bowl, combine calamari rings with lemon juice.
2. Marinate for 30 minutes, then drain in a colander.
3. Toss sweet potato fries with olive oil, paprika, garlic powder, smoked paprika (if using), salt, and pepper.
   - First dish: Mix flour and garlic powder.
   - Second dish: Whisk together egg whites and milk.
   - Third dish: Combine panko breadcrumbs, salt, and pepper.
4. Pat calamari rings dry and coat each in the flour mixture, then dip in the egg mixture, and finally coat with seasoned breadcrumbs.
5. Preheat the Ninja Foodi air fryer to 400°F.
6. Lightly spray Basket 1 with cooking spray and arrange calamari rings in a single layer.
7. In Basket 2, place the sweet potato fries.
8. Set Basket 1 (Crispy Calamari Rings) to 400°F for 10 minutes, shaking halfway through.
9. Set Basket 2 (Seasoned Sweet Potato Fries) to 400°F for 12 minutes, shaking halfway through.
10. Serve the crispy calamari rings hot with lemon wedges and your favorite dipping sauce.
11. Pair with the seasoned sweet potato fries for a complete and delicious meal.

CURRY ROASTED CHICKPEAS WITH SPICY ROASTED ALMONDS

Prep time: 5 minutes | **Cook time:15 minutes** | **Serves 2**

Curry Roasted Chickpeas:

- 1 (15-ounce) can chickpeas, drained and rinsed
- 2 teaspoons curry powder
- ¼ teaspoon kosher salt
- 1 tablespoon olive oil

Spicy Roasted Almonds:

- 1 cup raw almonds
- 1 tablespoon olive oil
- 1 teaspoon smoked paprika
- ½ teaspoon garlic powder
- ¼ teaspoon cayenne pepper
- ¼ teaspoon kosher salt

1. Drain and rinse the chickpeas thoroughly.
2. Spread chickpeas on paper towels. Cover with another paper towel and gently pat dry.
3. In a small bowl, mix curry powder and salt.
4. Transfer chickpeas to a medium bowl.
5. Sprinkle with the curry powder and salt mixture, stirring to coat evenly.
6. Drizzle with olive oil and toss to distribute.
7. In a bowl, combine almonds with olive oil, smoked paprika, garlic powder, cayenne pepper, and salt.
8. Toss thoroughly to coat evenly.
9. Preheat both baskets of the air fryer to 390°F.
10. In one basket, spread chickpeas in a single layer.
11. In the second basket, spread almonds in a single layer.
12. Shake both baskets halfway through cooking.
13. Ensure even roasting and crispiness.
14. Allow both chickpeas and almonds to cool completely before storing in airtight containers.

THYME SWEET POTATO CHIPS WITH GARLIC PARMESAN ZUCCHINI CHIPS

Prep time: 15 minutes | **Cook time: 15 minutes** | **Serves 2**

Thyme Sweet Potato Chips:

- 1 tablespoon olive oil
- 1 medium sweet potato, thinly sliced
- ¼ teaspoon dried thyme
- Kosher salt, to taste

Garlic Parmesan Zucchini Chips:

- 1 medium zucchini, thinly sliced
- 1 tablespoon olive oil
- 2 tablespoons grated Parmesan cheese
- ½ teaspoon garlic powder
- ¼ teaspoon dried oregano
- Kosher salt, to taste

1. Preheat both baskets of the air fryer to 390°F.
2. Lightly spray one air fryer basket with cooking spray.
3. Arrange sweet potato slices in a single layer.
4. Brush the slices with olive oil.
5. In a bowl, toss zucchini slices with olive oil, Parmesan cheese, garlic powder, oregano, and salt.
6. Lightly spray the second air fryer basket with cooking spray.
7. Arrange zucchini slices in a single layer.
8. Sweet Potato Chips: Air fry for 6 minutes.
9. Zucchini Chips: Air fry for the same duration.
10. For sweet potato chips, shake the slices and sprinkle with thyme and salt.
11. For zucchini chips, gently shake the basket.
12. Sweet potato chips are lightly browned and crisp
13. Zucchini chips are golden and crispy
14. Transfer both to serving plates.
15. Serve both chips warm.

CHAPTER 3: BREAKFAST RECIPES

EASY BAGELS

Prep time: 10 minutes | Cook time: 15 minutes | Serves 8

- 2 cups self-rising flour
- 2 cups non-fat plain Greek yogurt
- 2 large eggs,
- beaten (for egg wash, optional)
- ½ cup sesame seeds (optional)
- Cooking spray

1. In a medium mixing bowl, combine self-rising flour and Greek yogurt. Stir with a wooden spoon until a shaggy dough forms.
2. Transfer the dough to a lightly floured surface. Knead for 5 minutes until smooth.
3. Divide the dough into 8 equal pieces. Roll each piece into a rope and connect the ends to form a bagel shape.
4. If desired, brush each bagel with the beaten egg and sprinkle with sesame seeds for extra flavour and texture.
5. Preheat the Ninja Foodi 2-Basket Air Fryer to 360°F for 3 minutes.
6. Place crisper plates in both air fryer drawers.
7. Arrange 4 bagels in each drawer, ensuring they don't touch. This allows them to cook evenly.
8. Set Zone 1 (Basket 1) to Air Fry mode at 360°F for 15 minutes.
9. Press MATCH to synchronize the settings with Zone 2 (Basket 2).
10. Start the cooking process and allow the bagels to cook until golden brown and crisp.
11. Once the bagels are golden and crisp, remove them from the baskets and let them cool slightly before serving.

MORNING PATTIES

Prep time: 15 minutes | Cook time: 13 minutes | Serves 4

- 1 pound ground pork
- 1 pound ground turkey
- 2 teaspoons dried rubbed sage
- 2 teaspoons fennel seeds
- 2 teaspoons garlic powder
- 1 teaspoon paprika
- 1 teaspoon kosher salt
- 1 teaspoon dried thyme
- Cooking spray

1. In a large mixing bowl, combine ground pork and ground turkey. Mix thoroughly.
2. In a separate small bowl, mix sage, fennel seeds, paprika, salt, thyme, and garlic powder.
3. Sprinkle the seasoning mixture over the meat and mix until evenly distributed.
4. Divide mixture into 8 equal portions. Roll each portion into a thick patty, about 2 tablespoons each.
5. Spray the air fryer crisper plates with cooking oil.
6. Place 4 patties in Zone 1 basket and 4 patties in Zone 2 basket.
7. Set both baskets to Air Fry mode at 390°F for 13 minutes.
8. Press MATCH to synchronize settings between zones.
9. Start cooking and flip patties halfway through cooking time.
10. Serve hot and fresh.

WHITE WHEAT WALNUT BREAD

Prep time: 5 minutes | Cook time:25 minutes |Serves 8

- 1 cup lukewarm water
- 1 packet (2 ¼ teaspoons) yeast
- 1 tablespoon light brown sugar
- 2 cups whole-grain white wheat flour
- 1 large egg, room temperature, beaten
- 2 teaspoons olive oil
- ½ teaspoon kosher salt
- ½ cup chopped walnuts
- Cooking spray

1. In a small bowl, combine lukewarm water, yeast, and brown sugar. Stir lightly, then let it sit for about 5 minutes until slightly foamy.
2. Pour the yeast mixture over the flour and mix until smooth.
3. Add the beaten egg, olive oil, and salt. Stir with a wooden spoon for 2 minutes until well combined.
4. Gently fold in the chopped walnuts. The batter should be thick, similar to a quick bread consistency.
5. Thoroughly spray an air fryer baking pan with cooking spray. Pour the batter into the pan and smooth the top.
6. Let the batter rest and rise for 15 minutes to allow the yeast to activate further.
7. Preheat the Ninja Foodi 2-Basket Air Fryer to 360°F for 3 minutes.
8. If you have two pans and want to cook both simultaneously, divide the dough between two greased pans. Place one pan in Zone 1 and the other in Zone 2. Set both baskets to Air Fry mode at 360°F for 25 minutes.
9. After 25 minutes, insert a toothpick into the center of the bread. If it comes out with just a few moist crumbs, the bread is done.
10. Let the bread cool in the pan for 10 minutes before removing. Slice and serve warm.

QUICHE BREAKFAST PEPPERS

Prep time: 10 minutes | **Cook time: 15 minutes** | **Serves 4**

- 4 large eggs
- ½ teaspoon garlic powder
- 4 oz mozzarella cheese, shredded
- ½ cup ricotta cheese
- 2 bell peppers, halved and seeded
- ¼ cup baby spinach, chopped
- 1 oz Parmesan cheese, grated
- ¼ teaspoon dried parsley

1. In a medium bowl, whisk together eggs, ricotta cheese, garlic powder, parsley, Parmesan, and spinach.
2. Pour egg mixture evenly into bell pepper halves. Top with shredded mozzarella.
3. Insert crisper plates into both air fryer baskets. Place stuffed bell peppers in the baskets.
4. Set Zone 1 basket to Air Fry mode at 355°F for 15 minutes. Press MATCH to synchronize Zone 2 basket settings. Press START/STOP to begin cooking.

BREAKFAST CHEESE SANDWICH

Prep time: 10 minutes | **Cook time: 8 minutes** | **Serves: 2**

- 4 slices of bread
- 2 slices of provolone cheese
- 2 slices of Monterey Jack cheese
- 2 slices of cheddar cheese
- 2 tablespoons mayonnaise
- ¼ teaspoon dried basil
- ¼ teaspoon dried oregano

1. In a small bowl, combine the mayonnaise, dried basil, and dried oregano. Mix well.
2. Spread the seasoned mayonnaise on one side of two slices of bread.
3. Layer the cheddar cheese, provolone cheese, and Monterey Jack cheese on top of the prepared bread slices. Cover with the remaining bread slices to form sandwiches.
4. Insert the crisper plates into both baskets of the Ninja Foodi 2-Basket Air Fryer.
5. Place one sandwich in each basket.
6. Select Zone 1 basket, set it to Air Fry mode, and adjust the temperature to 390°F for 8 minutes. Press Match Zone 2 basket to copy the settings. Press Start/Stop to begin cooking. Turn the sandwiches halfway through the cooking time for even browning.
7. Once done, remove the sandwiches and let them cool slightly before serving.

BLUEBERRIES MUFFINS

Prep time: 15 minutes | **Cook time:** 15 minutes | Serves 2

- 2 large eggs
- 1/3 cup granulated sugar
- 1/3 cup vegetable oil
- 4 tablespoons water
- 1 teaspoon lemon zest
- ¼ teaspoon vanilla extract
- ½ teaspoon baking powder
- 1 cup all-purpose flour
- 1 cup fresh blueberries
- Pinch of salt
- Muffin liners

1. Prepare 4 oven-safe ramekins with muffin liners.
2. In a large mixing bowl, whisk together eggs, sugar, oil, water, vanilla extract, and lemon zest until well combined.
3. In a separate bowl, mix flour, baking powder, and salt.
4. Gradually add dry ingredients to wet ingredients, stirring until just combined.
5. Divide batter evenly among prepared ramekins.
6. Top each muffin with fresh blueberries.
7. Place 2 ramekins in each air fryer basket.
8. Set Zone 1 basket to Air Fry mode at 350°F for 15 minutes.
9. Press MATCH to synchronize Zone 2 basket settings.
10. If muffins are not done, cook for an additional 1-2 minutes.
11. Carefully remove and serve warm.

GARLIC BREAD

Prep time: 7 minutes | Cook time: 10 minutes | Serves 4

- ½ loaf of French bread or Italian bread
- 3 tablespoons unsalted butter, softened
- 3 garlic cloves, minced
- ½ teaspoon Italian seasoning
- Pinch of red pepper flakes

Optional Toppings:

- ¼ cup shredded mozzarella cheese
- Freshly grated Parmesan cheese
- Chopped fresh parsley

1. Slice bread horizontally to fit inside the air fryer baskets.
2. In a small bowl, combine softened butter, minced garlic, Italian seasoning, and red pepper flakes.
3. Evenly brush the garlic butter mixture over the bread.
4. Place a crisper plate in each air fryer drawer. Arrange bread pieces in the drawers.
5. Set Zone 1 basket to Air Fry mode at 360°F for 6 minutes. Press MATCH to synchronize Zone 2 basket settings. Press START/STOP to begin cooking.
6. Remove garlic bread from air fryer, slice, and serve immediately.

BREAKFAST POTATOES

Prep time: 5 minutes | Cook time:20 minutes |Serves 6

- 3 russet potatoes, scrubbed
- 1 teaspoon garlic powder
- 1 teaspoon onion powder
- 2 teaspoons kosher salt
- 1 teaspoon freshly ground black pepper
- 1 tablespoon olive oil
- ½ red bell pepper, diced

1. Wash and scrub potatoes. Cut into 1-inch bite-sized pieces, leaving skin on.
2. Pat potatoes dry with paper towels and transfer to a large mixing bowl.
3. Add garlic powder, onion powder, salt, pepper, and olive oil. Toss to coat evenly.
4. Mix in diced red bell pepper.
5. Preheat both air fryer zones to 380°F for 3 minutes.
6. Line air fryer baskets with parchment paper.
7. Spread potatoes in a single layer across both baskets.
8. Cook for 15-20 minutes, shaking baskets halfway through for even cooking.
9. Serve hot directly from the air fryer baskets.

EGG WHITE MUFFINS

Prep time: 15 minutes | Cook time: 22 minutes | Serves 8

- 4 slices center-cut bacon, chopped
- 4 ounces baby bella mushrooms, roughly chopped
- 2 ounces sun-dried tomatoes, chopped
- 2 tablespoons sliced black olives
- 2 tablespoons grated Parmesan cheese
- 2 tablespoons shredded mozzarella cheese
- ¼ teaspoon freshly ground black pepper
- 3/4 cup liquid egg whites
- 2 tablespoons liquid egg whites
- Cooking spray

1. In a skillet, cook bacon and mushrooms over medium heat until bacon is crispy, about 6-8 minutes.
2. In a large mixing bowl, combine 3/4 cup egg whites, sun-dried tomatoes, olives, Parmesan, mozzarella, and black pepper.
3. Add cooked bacon and mushrooms to the egg white mixture. Stir to combine.
4. Lightly spray a muffin tin with cooking spray.
5. Divide the mixture evenly among muffin cups, filling each about 3/4 full.
6. Top each muffin with an additional 2 tablespoons of egg whites.
7. Place half the muffin tin in each air fryer basket.
8. Set Zone 1 basket to Air Fry mode at 390°F for 22 minutes.
9. Press MATCH to synchronize Zone 2 basket settings.
10. Press START/STOP to begin cooking.
11. Once done, carefully remove muffins and serve.

CHAPTER 4: POULTRY MAINS RECIPES

SPICY CHICKEN

Prep time: 12 minutes | Cook time: 35-40 minutes | Serves 4

- 4 chicken thighs
- 4 chicken legs
- 2 cups buttermilk
- 2 cups flour
- Salt and black pepper, to taste
- 2 tbsp garlic powder
- ½ tsp onion powder
- 1 tsp poultry seasoning
- 1 tsp cumin
- 2 tbsp paprika
- 1 tbsp olive oil

1. Place the buttermilk in a large bowl and soak the chicken thighs and legs for 2 hours.
2. In a separate bowl, combine flour, all seasonings, and olive oil to form a coating mixture.
3. Remove the chicken from the buttermilk, allowing excess to drip off, and dredge each piece in the flour mixture.
4. Repeat for all pieces and arrange them in both air fryer baskets.
5. Set each basket to ROAST mode at 350°F for 35-40 minutes.
6. Once cooked, remove the chicken and serve hot.

CRISPY CHICKEN STRIPS

Prep time: 8 minutes | Cook time:15 minutes |Serves 4

- 1 pound chicken tenderloins
- ¼ teaspoon crushed red pepper flakes
- ½ teaspoon salt
- ½ cup grated Parmesan cheese
- ½ cup panko breadcrumbs
- ¼ cup butter, cubed

1. Combine breadcrumbs, Parmesan cheese, and crushed red pepper flakes in a shallow dish.
2. Melt butter in another shallow dish using a microwave.
3. Sprinkle salt over the chicken tenderloins.
4. Dip each chicken strip into melted butter, then coat thoroughly with the breadcrumb mixture.
5. Grease the baskets of Zone 1 basket and Zone 2 basket in the Ninja Foodi 2-Basket Air Fryer.
6. Preheat both baskets on Air Fry mode at 400°F for 5 minutes.
7. Arrange the chicken strips in both baskets.
8. Air fry for 7 minutes, flipping the chicken halfway through the cooking time.
9. Remove from the air fryer and serve immediately.

GINGERED CHICKEN DRUMSTICKS

Prep time: **10 minutes** | **Cook time:**25 minutes |**Serves 6**

- ½ cup full-fat coconut milk
- 4 tsp fresh ginger, minced
- 4 tsp galangal, minced
- 2 tsp ground turmeric
- Salt, to taste
- 6 chicken drumsticks (6 oz each)

1. In a large bowl, mix coconut milk, ginger, galangal, turmeric, and salt.
2. Add the drumsticks, coating them thoroughly. Cover and refrigerate for 6-8 hours.
3. Grease the baskets of both Zone 1 basket and Zone 2 basket of the Ninja Foodi 2-Basket Air Fryer.
4. Preheat each zone by selecting AIR FRY at 375°F for 5 minutes.
5. Arrange three drumsticks in each basket. Insert the baskets and set the timer for 25 minutes.
6. Once cooked, remove the drumsticks and serve hot.

CHICKEN WINGS

Prep time: **10 minutes** | **Cook time:** **35 minutes** |**Serves 3**

- 1 pound whole chicken wings
- 1 teaspoon garlic powder
- ½ teaspoon garlic salt
- ¼ teaspoon cayenne pepper
- ¼ teaspoon baking soda
- ¼ teaspoon ground allspice
- ¼ teaspoon black pepper
- ½ teaspoon mustard powder
- ½ teaspoon ground ginger
- ½ teaspoon ground nutmeg

1. In a large bowl, mix together all of the spices: garlic powder, garlic salt, cayenne pepper, baking soda, ground allspice, black pepper, mustard powder, ground ginger, and ground nutmeg.
2. Cut the chicken wings into sections (flats and drumettes), then coat them thoroughly in the spice mixture.
3. Lightly grease both baskets of the Ninja Foodi 2-Basket Air Fryer with cooking spray.
4. Preheat both baskets to 300°F for 5 minutes in Air Fry mode.
5. Divide the coated chicken wings evenly between the two baskets, ensuring they are not overcrowded.
6. Air fry the wings for 30–35 minutes, flipping halfway through for even cooking and crispiness.
7. Remove the chicken wings from the air fryer and serve hot.

CHICKEN CAPRESE

Prep time: 10 minutes | Cook time: 10 minutes | Serves: 4

- 4 chicken breast cutlets
- 1 teaspoon Italian seasoning
- 1 teaspoon salt
- ½ teaspoon black pepper
- 4 slices fresh mozzarella cheese
- 1 large tomato, sliced
- Fresh basil leaves and balsamic vinegar for garnish

1. Pat the chicken cutlets dry with a kitchen towel.
2. Season both sides of the chicken with Italian seasoning, salt, and black pepper.
3. Place two chicken cutlets in each air fryer basket.
4. Insert Basket 1 into Zone 1 basket and Basket 2 into Zone 2 basket of the Ninja Foodi 2-Basket Air Fryer.
5. Select "Air Fry" mode for Zone 1 basket at 375°F for 10 minutes.
6. Use the "MATCH COOK" function to apply the same settings to Zone 2 basket.
7. Press the START/PAUSE button to start cooking.
8. After 10 minutes, top each chicken cutlet with a slice of mozzarella and tomato.
9. Return the baskets to the air fryer and cook for an additional 5 minutes.
10. Garnish with fresh basil and a drizzle of balsamic vinegar. Serve warm.

CHICKEN NUGGETS

Prep time: 5 minutes | Cook time:10 minutes |Serves 4

- 1 pound ground chicken breast
- 1½ teaspoons salt, divided
- ¾ teaspoon ground black pepper, divided
- 1½ cups plain bread crumbs, divided
- 2 large eggs
- Cooking spray

1. Preheat the air fryer to 400°F.
2. In a large bowl, combine the ground chicken, 1 teaspoon of salt, ½ teaspoon of black pepper, and ½ cup of bread crumbs. Mix thoroughly.
3. In a small bowl, whisk the eggs.
4. In a separate bowl, mix the remaining 1 cup of bread crumbs, ½ teaspoon of salt, and ¼ teaspoon of black pepper.
5. Scoop 1 tablespoon of the chicken mixture and shape it into a nugget.
6. Dip each nugget into the beaten eggs, allowing any excess to drip off, then roll in the bread crumb mixture.
7. Repeat with the remaining chicken mixture to make about 20 nuggets.
8. Place 10 nuggets in Basket 1 and 10 nuggets in Basket 2, ensuring they are not overcrowded.
9. Set Zone 1 and Zone 2 to 400°F for 10 minutes.
10. Press MATCH to synchronise both baskets and start cooking.
11. Flip the nuggets halfway through cooking for even browning.
12. Remove the nuggets from the air fryer baskets and serve warm.

SESAME GINGER CHICKEN

Prep time: 10 minutes | Cook time: 30 minutes | Serves 4

- 4 oz green beans
- 1 tbsp canola oil
- 1½ lbs boneless, skinless chicken breasts
- ⅓ cup sesame-ginger sauce
- Kosher salt, to taste
- Black pepper, to taste

1. Toss green beans with salt and pepper in a mixing bowl.
2. Insert crisper plates into both drawers. Place the green beans in Zone 1 basket and the chicken breasts in Zone 2 basket.
3. Select AIR FRY mode for Zone 1 basket, set to 390°F for 10 minutes. For Zone 2 basket, set AIR FRY to 390°F for 18 minutes. Use the SYNC function and press START/STOP.
4. Pause cooking when Zone 2 basket reaches 9 minutes. Remove the chicken, toss it in sesame-ginger sauce, and return to the air fryer to resume cooking.
5. When cooking is complete, serve chicken with green beans immediately.

CHICKEN SKEWERS

Prep time: 10 minutes | Cook time: 15 minutes | Serves 4

- 2 pounds chicken thighs, cut into cubes
- 3 tablespoons fresh lime juice
- ¼ cup coconut milk
- 2 tablespoons Thai red curry paste
- 2 tablespoons maple syrup
- ½ cup tamari soy sauce

1. In a large bowl, combine chicken cubes, lime juice, coconut milk, Thai red curry paste, maple syrup, and tamari soy sauce. Stir well.
2. Cover the bowl and refrigerate for at least 2 hours to marinate.
3. Thread the marinated chicken pieces onto pre-soaked skewers.
4. Place a crisper plate in each air fryer basket and arrange the chicken skewers evenly in both baskets.
5. Insert Basket 1 into Zone 1 basket and Basket 2 into Zone 2 basket.
6. Select "Air Fry" mode for Zone 1 basket at 360°F and set the timer for 15 minutes.
7. Use the "MATCH COOK" function to apply the same settings to Zone 2 basket.
8. Press the START/PAUSE button to begin cooking.
9. Serve the skewers hot and enjoy.

CHAPTER 5: BEEF, LAMB, AND PORK RECIPES

STEAK FAJITAS

Prep time: 5 minutes | **Cook time:** 20 minutes | **Serves** 4

- 1 pound beef flank steak, cut into ½-inch strips
- 1 red bell pepper, cut into thin strips
- 1 green bell pepper, cut into thin strips
- ½ cup sweet corn kernels
- 1 shallot, thinly sliced
- 2 tablespoons fajita seasoning
- Kosher salt and freshly ground black pepper
- 2 tablespoons olive oil
- 8 flour tortillas
- Optional toppings: sour cream, guacamole, salsa

1. Preheat the air fryer to 380°F.
2. In a large bowl, combine flank steak strips, bell peppers, corn, shallot, fajita seasoning, salt, pepper, and olive oil. Toss until evenly coated.
3. Basket 1: Transfer the steak and vegetable mixture to Basket 1, spreading it in an even layer.
4. Basket 2: Place the flour tortillas in Basket 2. Arrange them in a single layer, ensuring they're not overlapping. (You can fold them or stack them if needed.)
5. Cook for 9-11 minutes, shaking Basket 1 halfway through cooking to ensure even browning. The tortillas should heat through in Basket 2 as the steak and vegetables cook.
6. Once the cooking is done, warm the tortillas in a skillet or microwave if needed for a few seconds.
7. Serve the hot fajita mixture with the warm tortillas and optional toppings, such as sour cream, guacamole, and salsa.

BLOSSOM BBQ PORK CHOPS

Prep time: 5 minutes | **Cook time:** 20 minutes | **Serves** 2

- 2 tablespoons cherry preserves
- 1 tablespoon honey
- 1 tablespoon Dijon mustard
- 2 teaspoons light brown sugar
- 1 teaspoon Worcestershire sauce
- 1 tablespoon fresh lime juice
- 1 tablespoon olive oil
- 2 garlic cloves, minced
- 1 tablespoon chopped fresh parsley
- 2 pork chops

1. In a medium bowl, whisk together the cherry preserves, honey, Dijon mustard, brown sugar, Worcestershire sauce, lime juice, olive oil, and minced garlic.
2. Add the pork chops to the marinade, turning to coat completely. Cover and refrigerate for 30 minutes to allow the flavours to meld.
3. Basket 1: Preheat the air fryer to 350°F. Lightly spray the basket with nonstick cooking spray. Place the marinated pork chops in Basket 1.
4. Basket 2: While the pork chops are marinating, prepare a side dish such as roasted potatoes, sweet potato wedges, or vegetables like carrots or Brussels sprouts. Toss with olive oil, salt, and pepper to taste.
5. Place Basket 1 with the pork chops and Basket 2 with the side dish into the air fryer.
6. Air fry for 12 minutes, turning the pork chops once halfway through cooking. Check that the side dish is cooked to your liking (adjust cooking time as needed).
7. Transfer the pork chops to a cutting board and let rest for 5 minutes before serving. Garnish with chopped parsley.

GROUND BEEF

Prep time: **5 minutes** | **Cook time:** **9 minutes** | **Serves** 4

- 1 pound ground beef (70/30 lean-to-fat ratio)
- ¼ cup water
- 1 teaspoon kosher salt
- ½ teaspoon freshly ground black pepper
- 1 teaspoon garlic powder

1. Basket 1: Preheat the air fryer to 400°F.
2. In a medium bowl, combine ground beef, water, salt, black pepper, and garlic powder. Mix thoroughly.
3. Lightly grease a 6-inch round cake pan. Press the beef mixture into an even layer in the pan.
4. Place the pan with the beef in Basket 1.
5. Basket 2: Prepare a complementary side dish (e.g., roasted vegetables, fries, or a side of crispy Brussels sprouts) and place it in Basket 2.
6. Cook the ground beef for 5 minutes.
7. After 5 minutes, open the air fryer and break up the beef with a spatula. Redistribute the beef evenly.
8. Continue cooking for 2 minutes.
9. Remove the pan, drain any excess fat, and return to the air fryer.
10. Cook for an additional 2 minutes or until the beef is completely browned, with no pink remaining.
11. Drain the beef and serve with the side dish from Basket 2.

PEPPERED STEAK BITES

Prep time: 5 minutes | Cook time: 14 minutes | Serves 4

- 1 pound sirloin steak, cut into 1-inch cubes
- ½ teaspoon kosher salt
- 1 teaspoon freshly ground black pepper
- 2 teaspoons Worcestershire sauce
- ½ teaspoon garlic powder
- ¼ teaspoon red pepper flakes
- ¼ cup chopped fresh parsley

1. Preheat both baskets of the Ninja Foodi 2-Basket Air Fryer to 390°F.
2. In a large mixing bowl, combine the steak cubes with salt, black pepper, Worcestershire sauce, garlic powder, and red pepper flakes. Toss until the steak is evenly coated with the seasoning.
3. Divide the seasoned steak cubes evenly between both air fryer baskets. Ensure they are spread out in a single layer for even cooking.
4. Set both baskets to cook for 10 to 14 minutes at 390°F, depending on your preferred level of doneness. Start at the 8-minute mark, shaking each basket or using tongs to turn the steak bites every 2 minutes to ensure even cooking.
5. Once the steak reaches your desired level of doneness, transfer it to a serving bowl.
6. Sprinkle with chopped fresh parsley and let rest for 5 minutes before serving.

BALSAMIC BEEF & VEGGIE SKEWERS

Prep time: 5 minutes | **Cook time:** 25 minutes | **Serves** 4

- 2 tablespoons balsamic vinegar
- 2 teaspoons olive oil
- ½ teaspoon dried oregano
- Kosher salt and freshly ground black pepper to taste
- ¾ pound round steak, cut into 1-inch cubes
- 1 red bell pepper, cut into 1-inch pieces
- 1 yellow bell pepper, cut into 1-inch pieces
- 1 cup cherry tomatoes

1. Preheat the air fryer to 390°F.
2. In a large bowl, whisk together balsamic vinegar, olive oil, oregano, salt, and black pepper.
3. Add steak cubes to the marinade and toss to coat. Let sit for 10 minutes.
4. Skewer the marinated steak cubes, red and yellow bell peppers, and cherry tomatoes onto 8 metal or pre-soaked wooden skewers, alternating ingredients as you go.
5. Basket 1: Place the skewers in Basket 1, ensuring they are not crowded.
6. Basket 2: If you prefer, you can place any extra vegetables or tomatoes in Basket 2 for a quick side.
7. Air fry for 5-7 minutes, turning the skewers halfway through cooking. The beef should be golden brown and cooked through, and the vegetables should be tender.
8. Serve the skewers immediately.

HONEY GARLIC PORK CHOPS

Prep time: 5 minutes | **Cook time:15 minutes** | **Serves** 4

- 4 pork chops
- Kosher salt and freshly ground black pepper
- 4 tablespoons olive oil
- 4 garlic cloves, minced
- 2 tablespoons sweet chili sauce
- 4 tablespoons fresh lemon juice
- ½ cup honey

1. Season the pork chops with kosher salt and black pepper on both sides.
2. Preheat the air fryer to 400°F.
3. Basket 1: Place the pork chops in Basket 1. Air fry for 7 minutes on one side.
4. Basket 2: While the pork chops are cooking, prepare the sauce: In a skillet over medium heat, warm the olive oil. Add the minced garlic and cook for 30 seconds.
5. Stir in the sweet chili sauce, lemon juice, and honey. Simmer for 10 minutes, stirring occasionally until the sauce thickens.
6. After the first 7 minutes, flip the pork chops and place them in Basket 2. Continue cooking for another 7 minutes or until the internal temperature reaches 145°F.
7. Once the pork chops are done, transfer them to the skillet with the sauce and toss to coat.
8. Serve the pork chops hot, drizzled with the honey garlic sauce.

ITALIAN MEATBALLS

Prep time: 5 minutes | Cook time: 12 minutes | Serves 4

- 12 ounces lean ground beef
- 4 ounces Italian sausage, casings removed
- ½ cup plain breadcrumbs
- 1 cup freshly grated Parmesan cheese
- 1 large egg
- 2 tablespoons whole milk
- 2 teaspoons Italian seasoning
- ½ teaspoon onion powder
- ½ teaspoon garlic powder
- Pinch of red pepper flakes
- Nonstick cooking spray

1. In a large mixing bowl, combine the ground beef, Italian sausage, breadcrumbs, Parmesan cheese, egg, milk, Italian seasoning, onion powder, garlic powder, and red pepper flakes.
2. Mix thoroughly using your hands until well combined, being careful not to overmix.
3. Divide the mixture and roll into 24 evenly sized meatballs, about 1-inch in diameter.
4. Basket 1: Lightly spray the basket with nonstick cooking spray. Place the meatballs in Basket 1, ensuring they are not touching.
5. Basket 2: Prepare a simple side dish, such as roasted vegetables (e.g., bell peppers, zucchini, or cherry tomatoes) or garlic bread. Lightly season with olive oil, salt, pepper, and herbs of your choice.
6. Preheat the air fryer to 360°F.
7. Place Basket 1 with the meatballs and Basket 2 with the side dish in the air fryer.
8. Air fry for 12 minutes, shaking the meatball basket every 4 minutes for even cooking. Keep an eye on the side dish to ensure it is also cooked to your liking.
9. Use a meat thermometer to verify the internal temperature of the meatballs reaches 165°F.
10. Let the meatballs rest for 2-3 minutes before serving with your side dish.

CHAPTER 6: FISH AND SEAFOOD RECIPES

GARLICKY SEA BASS WITH ROOT VEGETABLES

Prep time: 5 minutes | Cook time: 25 minutes | Serves 4

- 1 large carrot, small dice
- 1 parsnip, small dice
- ½ rutabaga, small dice
- ½ turnip, small dice
- ¼ cup olive oil
- Celery salt
- 4 sea bass fillets (6 ounces each)
- ½ teaspoon onion powder
- 2 garlic cloves, minced
- 1 lemon, thinly sliced
- Kosher salt and freshly ground black pepper

1. Preheat the air fryer to 380°F.
2. In a medium bowl, toss diced carrots, parsnips, turnips, and rutabaga with 2 tablespoons olive oil, a pinch of celery salt, and black pepper.
3. Pat the sea bass fillets dry with paper towels. Brush with the remaining olive oil and season with onion powder, salt, and pepper.
4. For Basket 1: Place the sea bass fillets, sprinkle minced garlic over the top, and arrange lemon slices on top of each fillet.
5. For Basket 2: Distribute the prepared root vegetables around and on top of the fish, ensuring they're evenly spread out for even cooking.
6. Air fry for 15 minutes, or until the fish is opaque and flakes easily with a fork, and the vegetables are tender.
7. Carefully transfer the fish and vegetables to serving plates and serve immediately.

CATFISH NUGGETS

Prep time: 5 minutes | Cook time: 7 minutes per batch | Serves 4

- 2 medium catfish fillets, cut into bite-sized chunks
- Kosher salt and freshly ground black pepper
- 2 large eggs
- 2 tablespoons whole milk
- ½ cup cornstarch
- 1 cup panko breadcrumbs
- Cooking spray or olive oil spray

1. Season catfish chunks with salt and pepper.
2. Set up a breading station:
   - First bowl: cornstarch
   - Second bowl: eggs whisked with milk
   - Third bowl: panko breadcrumbs
3. Dredge each catfish chunk in cornstarch, shaking off excess.
4. Dip in egg wash, allowing excess to drip off.
5. Roll in panko breadcrumbs, pressing gently to coat evenly.
6. Lightly spray breaded nuggets with cooking spray.
7. For Basket 1: Place half of the breaded catfish nuggets in the first basket in a single layer, ensuring space between pieces.
8. For Basket 2: Place the remaining nuggets in the second basket.
9. Air fry both baskets at 390°F for 4 minutes, then flip the nuggets and cook an additional 3 minutes, or until golden brown and fish flakes easily.
10. Serve hot and enjoy!

CHEESY SALMON-STUFFED AVOCADOS

Prep time: 5 minutes | **Cook time:** 20 minutes | **Serves** 2

- ¼ cup apple cider vinegar
- 1 teaspoon granulated sugar
- ¼ cup thinly sliced red onions
- 2 ounces cream cheese, softened
- 1 tablespoon capers, drained
- 2 ripe avocados, halved and pitted
- 4 ounces smoked salmon, flaked
- ¼ teaspoon dried dill
- 2 cherry tomatoes, halved
- 1 tablespoon fresh cilantro, chopped

1. Prepare the pickled onions: In a small saucepan, combine apple cider vinegar and sugar. Bring to a simmer over medium heat for 4 minutes.
2. Remove from heat, add sliced red onions, and let sit until cool. Drain before using.
3. In a small bowl, mix cream cheese and capers. Refrigerate until ready to use.
4. Preheat the air fryer to 350°F.
5. For Basket 1: Place the avocado halves, cut-side up, in one basket. Air fry for 4 minutes.
6. For Basket 2: While the avocados cook, prepare the toppings by flaking the smoked salmon and chopping the cherry tomatoes.
7. Once the avocado halves are ready, transfer them to serving plates. Top each with the cream cheese-caper mixture, flaked smoked salmon, dried dill, pickled red onions, cherry tomato halves, and chopped cilantro.
8. Serve immediately.

PANKO-BREADED COD FILLETS

Prep time: **5 minutes** | **Cook time:** **20 minutes** | **Serves** **2**

- 1 lemon, zested and juiced
- ½ cup panko breadcrumbs
- Kosher salt and freshly ground black pepper
- 1 tablespoon Dijon mustard
- 1 tablespoon unsalted butter, melted
- 2 cod fillets (6 ounces each)
- Nonstick cooking spray

1. Preheat the air fryer to 350°F. Lightly spray both baskets with nonstick cooking spray.
2. In a shallow bowl, combine panko breadcrumbs, lemon zest, salt, and pepper.
3. In another small bowl, whisk together Dijon mustard, melted butter, and lemon juice.
4. Brush each cod fillet with the mustard mixture, then press into the panko mixture, coating evenly.
5. For Basket 1: Place 1 cod fillet into the first basket.
6. For Basket 2: Place the second cod fillet into the second basket.
7. Air fry both baskets for 10 minutes, or until the cod is opaque and flakes easily with a fork.
8. Serve immediately with a lemon wedge.

BUTTERED MAHI-MAHI

Prep time: **15 minutes** | **Cook time:** **22 minutes** |**Serves** **4**

- 4 mahi-mahi fillets (6 ounces each)
- Kosher salt and freshly ground black pepper
- Cooking spray
- ⅔ cup unsalted butter
- Fresh parsley, chopped (for garnish)
- Lemon wedges (for serving)

1. Preheat Ninja Foodi 2-Basket Air Fryer to 350°F.
2. Season mahi-mahi fillets with salt and pepper.
3. Lightly spray the crisper plates with cooking spray.
4. Place two fillets in each crisper plate.
5. Set Zone 1 basket to Air Fry mode at 390°F for 17 minutes.
6. Press "MATCH" to copy settings to Zone 2 basket.
7. Start cooking by pressing START/STOP button.
8. While fish cooks, prepare brown butter:
   - Melt butter in a small saucepan over medium heat
   - Cook, stirring occasionally, until butter turns light brown and develops a nutty aroma (about 5 minutes)
   - Remove from heat
9. Once fish is done, transfer to serving plates.
10. Drizzle brown butter over fillets.
11. Garnish with chopped parsley and serve with lemon wedges.

CRISPY HADDOCK WITH AIR FRYER CHIPS

Prep time: 10 minutes | Cook time:12 minutes |Serves 4

For the Haddock:

- 4 haddock fillets
- ½ cup all-purpose flour
- 6 tablespoons mayonnaise
- 2 large eggs
- 3 cups plain breadcrumbs
- Kosher salt and freshly ground black pepper, to taste
- Cooking spray or olive oil spray

For the Chips (side dish for Basket 2):

- 4 large potatoes, peeled and cut into thick fries
- 1-2 tablespoons olive oil
- Kosher salt, to taste
- Freshly ground black pepper, to taste
- Optional: garlic powder or paprika for extra flavour

1. Set up a breading station with three shallow bowls:
   - First bowl: flour
   - Second bowl: mayonnaise whisked with eggs
   - Third bowl: breadcrumbs seasoned with salt and pepper
2. Pat haddock fillets dry with paper towels.
3. Coat each fillet lightly with flour, shaking off excess.
4. Dip floured fish in the egg-mayo mixture.
5. Thoroughly coat in seasoned breadcrumbs, pressing gently to adhere.
6. Lightly spray the breaded fillets with cooking spray.
7. Toss the potato fries with olive oil, salt, pepper, and any optional seasonings like garlic powder or paprika.
8. Ensure the fries are evenly coated.
9. Preheat the Ninja Foodi 2-Basket Air Fryer to 350°F.
10. Place the breaded haddock fillets in one basket (Basket 1) in a single layer.
11. Add the prepared chips to the second basket (Basket 2), ensuring they're evenly spread out.
12. Cook the fish and chips at the same time for 10-12 minutes. Shake the chips halfway through the cooking time.
13. Flip the haddock fillets at 5-6 minutes to ensure even cooking and crispiness on both sides.
14. Cook until the fish is golden brown and flakes easily with a fork, and the chips are crispy and golden.
15. Serve the crispy haddock with the freshly made chips, along with tartar sauce or lemon wedges on the side.

COCONUT SHRIMP WITH ASIAN-INSPIRED CUCUMBER SALAD

Prep time: 10 minutes | Cook time:6 minutes |Serves 6

For the Coconut Shrimp:

- 1 pound large shrimp, peeled and deveined
- Kosher salt and freshly ground black pepper
- ½ cup all-purpose flour
- 2 large eggs, beaten
- ¼ cup plain breadcrumbs
- 1 cup sweetened coconut flakes
- Cooking spray or olive oil spray
- Sweet chili sauce for dipping (optional)

For the Asian-Inspired Cucumber Salad (Side Dish for Basket 2):

- 2 medium cucumbers, thinly sliced
- 1 tablespoon rice vinegar
- 1 teaspoon sesame oil
- ½ teaspoon soy sauce
- ¼ teaspoon sugar
- ½ teaspoon sesame seeds (optional)
- Fresh cilantro, chopped (optional)

1. In a small bowl, whisk together the rice vinegar, sesame oil, soy sauce, and sugar until the sugar dissolves.
2. Place the thinly sliced cucumbers in a large bowl. Pour the dressing over the cucumbers and toss to coat.
3. Sprinkle with sesame seeds and chopped cilantro, if desired. Set aside to allow the flavours to meld.
4. Pat the shrimp dry with paper towels and season with salt and pepper.
5. Set up a breading station with three bowls:
   - First bowl: flour
   - Second bowl: beaten eggs
   - Third bowl: mix of breadcrumbs and coconut flakes
6. Coat each shrimp in the flour, shaking off any excess, then dip it in the beaten eggs, and finally roll it in the coconut-breadcrumb mixture, pressing gently to coat. Lightly spray the breaded shrimp with cooking spray.
7. Preheat the Ninja Foodi 2-Basket Air Fryer to 400°F (200°C).
8. Place the breaded shrimp in one basket (Basket 1) in a single layer.
9. In the second basket (Basket 2), add the prepared cucumber salad. If you have a small dish or cup that fits within the second basket, you can place the salad in it to keep it fresh and prevent it from mixing with the shrimp.
10. Cook the coconut shrimp for 3 minutes per side, or until golden and crispy. Flip the shrimp halfway through.
11. If using a separate dish for the cucumber salad, you can simply serve it once the shrimp is done.
12. Serve the coconut shrimp hot with sweet chili sauce for dipping.
13. Plate the cucumber salad alongside the shrimp for a light and refreshing contrast.

LEMON-DILL SALMON WITH GREEN BEANS

Prep time: 5 minutes | **Cook time:** 15 minutes | **Serves** 4

- 4 wild-caught salmon fillets (6 ounces each)
- 4 tablespoons unsalted butter, softened
- 4 garlic cloves, minced
- ¼ cup fresh dill, chopped
- ¼ cup dry white wine
- Kosher salt and freshly ground black pepper, to taste
- 20 cherry tomatoes, halved
- 1 pound green beans, trimmed
- 1 lemon, thinly sliced
- 2 tablespoons fresh parsley, chopped

1. Preheat the Ninja Foodi air fryer to 390°F.
2. In a small bowl, combine softened butter, minced garlic, chopped dill, white wine, salt, and pepper.
3. Pat salmon fillets dry with paper towels and season lightly with salt and pepper.
4. Spread the herb butter evenly over the top of each salmon fillet.
5. For Basket 1: Place 2 salmon fillets in the first basket.
6. For Basket 2: Place the remaining 2 salmon fillets in the second basket.
7. Surround the salmon in both baskets with green beans and cherry tomatoes.
8. Top each salmon fillet with lemon slices.
9. Air fry both baskets for 12-15 minutes, or until the salmon is cooked to your desired doneness and vegetables are tender.
10. Garnish with fresh parsley and serve with additional lemon slices on the side.

COD WITH CREAMY GARLIC PESTO SAUCE & ROASTED BABY POTATOES

Prep time: 10 minutes | Cook time:15 minutes |Serves 4

For the Cod with Creamy Garlic Pesto Sauce:

- 4 cod fillets (6 ounces each)
- 1 tablespoon extra-virgin olive oil
- 2 garlic cloves, minced
- ¼ cup basil pesto
- 3 tablespoons heavy cream
- Kosher salt and freshly ground black pepper, to taste
- Fresh basil leaves for garnish (optional)

For the Roasted Baby Potatoes (Side Dish for Basket 2):

- 1 pound baby potatoes, halved
- 1 tablespoon olive oil
- 1 teaspoon dried rosemary (or thyme)
- Kosher salt and freshly ground black pepper, to taste

1. In a small saucepan, heat olive oil over medium heat.
2. Add minced garlic and sauté for 30 seconds, stirring constantly to avoid burning.
3. Stir in the pesto and cream, then simmer for 5 minutes. Remove from heat and set aside to stay warm.
4. Toss the halved baby potatoes with olive oil, rosemary, salt, and pepper until evenly coated.
5. Set aside while you preheat the air fryer.
6. Preheat the Ninja Foodi 2-Basket Air Fryer to 350°F (175°C).
7. Place the cod fillets in one basket (Basket 1). Season with salt and pepper.
8. In the second basket (Basket 2), add the prepared baby potatoes in a single layer. Ensure the potatoes are evenly spaced out for even cooking.
9. Cook the cod fillets and baby potatoes at the same time for 10-12 minutes. Flip the fish fillets at 5-6 minutes, and shake the basket with the potatoes halfway through cooking.
10. The cod is done when it is opaque and flakes easily with a fork, and the potatoes should be crispy on the outside and tender on the inside.
11. Transfer the cod fillets to serving plates and spoon the creamy garlic pesto sauce over the top.
12. Serve alongside the roasted baby potatoes.
13. Garnish with fresh basil leaves, if desired.

CHAPTER 7:
VEGETABLES AND
SIDES RECIPES

GARLIC-HERB FRIED SQUASH

Prep time: 5 minutes | Cook time: 15 minutes | Serves 4

- 5 cups pattypan squash, halved (about 1 ¼ pounds)
- 1 tablespoon extra-virgin olive oil
- 2 garlic cloves, minced
- ½ teaspoon kosher salt
- ¼ teaspoon dried oregano
- ¼ teaspoon dried thyme
- ¼ teaspoon freshly ground black pepper
- 1 tablespoon fresh parsley, finely chopped

1. In a large bowl, combine olive oil, minced garlic, salt, oregano, thyme, and pepper.
2. Add squash to the bowl and toss to coat evenly.
3. Place crisper plates in both air fryer drawers.
4. Arrange squash in a single layer across both drawers.
5. Set Zone 1 basket to Air Fry mode at 360°F for 6 minutes.
6. Press Match button to sync Zone 2 basket settings.
7. Start cooking by pressing Start/Stop.
8. Once cooking is complete, sprinkle with fresh parsley.
9. Serve immediately.

ITALIAN STUFFED TOMATOES

Prep time: **10 minutes** | **Cook time:** **15 minutes** | **Serves 4**

- 4 medium ripe tomatoes
- 1 cup cooked brown rice
- 1/3 cup freshly grated Parmesan cheese
- ¼ cup crumbled goat cheese
- ¼ cup chopped toasted walnuts
- 2 tablespoons fresh basil, finely chopped (divided)
- 2 cloves garlic, minced
- ¼ cup Italian-seasoned breadcrumbs
- 1 tablespoon olive oil
- Olive oil cooking spray

1. Preheat the Ninja Foodi 2-Basket Air Fryer to 370°F for 5 minutes.
2. Prepare the tomatoes by cutting off the tops and carefully scooping out the flesh, leaving ¼- to ½-inch thick walls.
3. In a medium mixing bowl, combine the cooked rice, Parmesan cheese, goat cheese, walnuts, 1 tablespoon of basil, and minced garlic.
4. In a separate small bowl, mix the breadcrumbs with 1 tablespoon of olive oil.
5. Fill each tomato halfway with the rice mixture, then top with the prepared breadcrumb mixture.
6. Lightly spray both air fryer baskets with cooking spray.
7. Place the stuffed tomatoes in one basket and, in the other basket, add a side like crispy air fryer potatoes or roasted vegetables to cook simultaneously.
8. For potatoes or vegetables: Cut into bite-sized pieces, lightly coat with olive oil, salt, and pepper, and cook for 15 minutes at 370°F, shaking the basket halfway through.
9. Cook for 15 minutes, or until the tomatoes are tender and the breadcrumb topping is golden brown.
10. Remove both baskets from the air fryer, garnish the tomatoes with remaining fresh basil, and serve immediately with the side dish.

GREEN BEANS WITH BAKED POTATOES

Prep time: 15 minutes | Cook time: 45 minutes | Serves 2

- 2 cups fresh green beans, trimmed
- 2 large russet potatoes, cut into 1-inch cubes
- 3 tablespoons extra-virgin olive oil
- 1 teaspoon seasoned salt
- ½ teaspoon chili powder
- ⅛ teaspoon garlic powder
- ¼ teaspoon onion powder
- Fresh chopped parsley for garnish (optional)

1. In a large bowl, whisk together olive oil, seasoned salt, chili powder, garlic powder, and onion powder.
2. Toss green beans in half the seasoned oil mixture.
3. Toss potato cubes in remaining seasoned oil.
4. Transfer green beans to Zone 1 basket air fryer basket.
5. Place seasoned potato cubes in Zone 2 basket basket.
6. Press Sync button to coordinate cooking.
7. Cook until vegetables are tender and lightly crisp.
8. Garnish with fresh parsley before serving.

AIR-FRIED RADISHES

Prep time: 10 minutes | Cook time: 15 minutes | Serves 6

- 36 ounces radishes, quartered
- 3 tablespoons olive oil
- 1 tablespoon fresh oregano, finely chopped
- ¼ teaspoon kosher salt
- ⅛ teaspoon freshly ground black pepper

1. In a large mixing bowl, toss radishes with olive oil, black pepper, salt, and oregano until evenly coated.
2. Divide the seasoned radishes between the two baskets of the Ninja Foodi 2-Basket Air Fryer.
3. For Zone 1 basket, select the "Air Fry" mode and set the temperature to 375°F for 15 minutes.
4. Press the "MATCH COOK" button to apply the same settings to Zone 2 basket.
5. Press the START/PAUSE button to begin cooking.
6. Halfway through cooking, pause the air fryer and carefully shake or stir the radishes to ensure even browning.
7. Once cooking is complete, remove the radishes and serve immediately.

MEXICAN-SPICED CAULIFLOWER

Prep time: **10 minutes** | **Cook time:** **12 minutes** | **Serves** **4**

- 1 medium cauliflower head, cut into florets
- ½ teaspoon ground turmeric
- 1 teaspoon onion powder
- 2 teaspoons garlic powder
- 2 teaspoons dried parsley
- 1 lime, juiced
- 2 tablespoons olive oil
- 1 teaspoon chili powder
- 1 teaspoon ground cumin
- Kosher salt and freshly ground black pepper to taste

1. In a large mixing bowl, combine cauliflower florets with onion powder, garlic powder, parsley, olive oil, chili powder, turmeric, cumin, salt, and pepper. Toss until florets are evenly coated.
2. Insert the crisper plates into both baskets of the Ninja Foodi 2-Basket Air Fryer.
3. Divide the cauliflower florets evenly between the two baskets.
4. For Zone 1 basket, select "Air Fry" mode and set the temperature to 390°F for 12 minutes.
5. Press the "MATCH" button to apply the same settings to Zone 2 basket.
6. Press START to begin cooking. Midway through cooking, pause and stir the cauliflower to ensure even roasting.
7. Once cooking is complete, remove cauliflower from the air fryer and drizzle with fresh lime juice before serving.

BEANS & VEGGIE BURGERS

Prep time: 15 minutes | **Cook time:** 15 minutes | **Serves** 8

- 2 cups cooked pinto beans, drained and rinsed
- 4 cups boiled potatoes, peeled and mashed
- 2 cups fresh spinach, finely chopped
- 2 cups fresh mushrooms, finely chopped
- 4 teaspoons chili-lime seasoning
- Olive oil cooking spray

1. In a large mixing bowl, combine the pinto beans, mashed potatoes, chopped spinach, mushrooms, and chili-lime seasoning. Using clean hands, mix thoroughly until well combined.

2. Divide the mixture into 8 equal portions and shape into uniform patties, approximately ½-inch thick.

3. Lightly spray both sides of each patty with olive oil cooking spray.

4. Prepare the Ninja Foodi 2-Basket Air Fryer by lightly greasing both "Zone 1 basket" and "Zone 2 basket" baskets with cooking spray. Set both baskets to "Air Fry" mode and preheat to 370°F for 5 minutes.

5. After preheating, carefully arrange 4 patties in each basket, ensuring they are not overcrowded. Cook for 12-15 minutes, flipping the patties halfway through cooking time, until they are golden brown and heated through.

6. Remove patties from the air fryer and serve immediately while hot.

SPICY BUTTERNUT SQUASH

Prep time: 10 minutes | **Cook time:** 25 minutes | **Serves** 2

- 1 small butternut squash, peeled and cut into ¾-inch cubes
- 1 tablespoon extra-virgin olive oil
- ½ teaspoon garlic powder
- ½ teaspoon kosher salt
- ⅛ teaspoon freshly ground black pepper
- 1 teaspoon red pepper flakes

1. Preheat the Ninja Foodi 2-Basket Air Fryer to 400°F for 5 minutes.
2. Peel the butternut squash and cut it into uniform ¾-inch cubes to ensure even cooking.
3. In a large mixing bowl, combine the squash cubes with olive oil, garlic powder, salt, black pepper, and red pepper flakes. Toss thoroughly to ensure even seasoning.
4. Divide the seasoned squash between both air fryer baskets, spreading them in a single layer in each.
5. Cook for 20-25 minutes, shaking the baskets or turning the squash halfway through cooking to promote even browning.
6. Once the squash is golden and tender, remove from both baskets and serve immediately.

BUTTERED GREEN BEANS

Prep time: 10 minutes | **Cook time:** 10 minutes | **Serves** 6

- 24 ounces green beans, trimmed
- 4 tablespoons unsalted butter, melted
- Kosher salt and freshly ground black pepper to taste

1. Lightly grease both baskets of the Ninja Foodi 2-Basket Air Fryer with cooking spray or butter.
2. Select "Zone 1 basket" and rotate the dial to "Air Fry" mode.
3. Preheat the air fryer to 400°F for 5 minutes.
4. In a large mixing bowl, toss green beans with melted butter, salt, and pepper until evenly coated.
5. Divide green beans evenly between the two air fryer baskets.
6. Cook at 400°F for 10 minutes, pausing halfway through to flip or shake the beans for even cooking.
7. Once cooking is complete, remove green beans and serve hot.

ROASTED SWEET POTATOES & BRUSSELS SPROUTS

Prep time: 10 minutes | Cook time: 35 minutes | Serves 8

- 12 ounces sweet potatoes, cut into 1-inch cubes
- 2 tablespoons olive oil
- 5.3 ounces onion, roughly chopped
- 12.4 ounces Brussels sprouts, halved
- Kosher salt and freshly ground black pepper to taste

For the Glaze:

- ⅓ cup ketchup
- ½ cup balsamic vinegar
- 1 tablespoon Dijon mustard
- 2 tablespoons honey

1. In a large bowl, combine Brussels sprouts, olive oil, onion, sweet potatoes, salt, and pepper. Toss until vegetables are evenly coated.
2. Insert the crisper plates into both baskets of the Ninja Foodi 2-Basket Air Fryer.
3. Divide the vegetable mixture evenly between the two baskets.
4. For Zone 1 basket, select "Air Fry" mode and set the temperature to 390°F for 25 minutes.
5. Press the "MATCH" button to apply the same settings to Zone 2 basket.
6. Press START to begin cooking. Midway through cooking, pause and stir the vegetables to ensure even roasting.
7. While vegetables are cooking, prepare the glaze: In a small saucepan, combine balsamic vinegar, ketchup, honey, and Dijon mustard.
8. Simmer the glaze over medium heat for 5-10 minutes, stirring occasionally, until slightly thickened.
9. Once vegetables are done, transfer to a serving dish and drizzle with the prepared glaze.

CHAPTER 8: DESSERTS AND SWEETS

DATE OAT COOKIES

Prep time: 10 minutes | Cook time: 20 minutes | Serves 6

- ¼ cup unsalted butter, softened
- 2 ½ tablespoons whole milk
- ½ cup granulated sugar
- ½ teaspoon vanilla extract
- ½ teaspoon lemon zest
- ½ teaspoon ground cinnamon
- 3/4 cup all-purpose flour
- ¼ teaspoon kosher salt
- 3/4 cup rolled oats
- ¼ teaspoon baking soda
- ¼ teaspoon baking powder
- 2 tablespoons dates, finely chopped

1. Using an electric mixer, cream the butter until light and fluffy. Add milk, sugar, lemon zest, and vanilla extract. Mix until well combined.
2. In a separate bowl, whisk together cinnamon, flour, salt, oats, baking soda, and baking powder.
3. Gradually add the dry ingredients to the wet ingredients, stirring with a wooden spoon until just combined. Fold in the chopped dates.
4. Preheat the Ninja Foodi 2-Basket Air Fryer to 350°F.
5. Drop tablespoonfuls of batter onto a greased air fryer-safe baking pan, leaving space between each cookie.
6. Place the baking pans in each of the two baskets, ensuring the cookies are evenly spaced out.
7. Air fry for 6-8 minutes, or until the cookies are light golden brown. You can cook both baskets at the same time, making double the batch!
8. Allow cookies to cool completely before serving. Alternatively, store unused batter in the refrigerator for later use.

HOLIDAY PEPPERMINT CAKE

Prep time: 5 minutes | Cook time: 20 minutes | Serves 4

- 1 ½ cups all-purpose flour
- 3 large eggs
- ⅓ cup molasses
- ½ cup olive oil
- ½ cup unsweetened almond milk
- ½ teaspoon vanilla extract
- ½ teaspoon peppermint extract
- 1 teaspoon baking powder
- ½ teaspoon kosher salt

1. Preheat the Ninja Foodi 2-Basket Air Fryer to 380°F.
2. In a large mixing bowl, whisk together eggs and molasses until smooth.
3. Gradually mix in olive oil, almond milk, vanilla extract, and peppermint extract.
4. In a separate bowl, sift together flour, baking powder, and salt.
5. Slowly incorporate the dry ingredients into the wet ingredients, mixing until just combined.
6. Grease two air fryer-safe baking pans and divide the batter evenly between them.
7. Place one pan in each of the two air fryer baskets. Cook for 12-15 minutes, or until a toothpick inserted into the center comes out clean.
8. Allow both cakes to cool slightly before serving.

HONEY-ROASTED MIXED NUTS

Prep time: **5 minutes** | **Cook time:** **15 minutes** | **Serves** **8**

- ½ cup raw, shelled pistachios
- ½ cup raw almonds
- 1 cup raw walnuts
- 2 tablespoons water
- 2 tablespoons honey
- 1 tablespoon vegetable oil
- 2 tablespoons granulated sugar
- ½ teaspoon kosher salt

1. Preheat the Ninja Foodi 2-Basket Air Fryer to 300°F.
2. Lightly spray two air fryer-safe pans with cooking spray. Divide the pistachios, almonds, and walnuts evenly between the two pans.
3. Place one pan in each of the two air fryer baskets.
4. Cook for 15 minutes, shaking both baskets every 5 minutes to ensure even roasting.
5. While the nuts are roasting, prepare the honey syrup: In a small saucepan, combine water, honey, and vegetable oil. Simmer over medium heat, stirring constantly, until the mixture thickens and coats the back of a wooden spoon.
6. Once the nuts are done, transfer them to the saucepan and toss to coat evenly with the honey syrup.
7. Line a baking sheet with parchment paper. Spread the nuts in a single layer and sprinkle with sugar and salt.
8. Refrigerate for at least 2 hours to allow the coating to harden.
9. Store in an airtight container in the refrigerator.

BROWN SUGAR BAKED APPLES

Prep time: 5 minutes | Cook time: 15 minutes | Serves 4

- 3 small tart apples (preferably McIntosh)
- 4 tablespoons (½ stick) unsalted butter
- 6 tablespoons light brown sugar
- Ground cinnamon
- Kosher salt

1. Preheat the Ninja Foodi 2-Basket Air Fryer to 400°F.
2. Wash the apples and cut them in half horizontally (across their equator). Using a melon baller, carefully remove the cores, keeping the apple halves intact.
3. Place the apple halves cut-side up in each air fryer basket, ensuring space between the halves in both baskets.
4. Divide the butter evenly among the apple cavities (about 2 teaspoons per half).
5. Sprinkle each apple half with 1 tablespoon of brown sugar, a pinch of ground cinnamon, and a small pinch of salt.
6. Air fry for 15 minutes, or until the apples are soft and the sugar has caramelized. You can cook both baskets at the same time for faster results.
7. Using a nonstick-safe spatula, transfer the apples to a wire rack. Let them cool for 10 minutes before serving.

CHOCOLATE RUM BROWNIES

Prep time: 5 minutes | Cook time: 30 minutes | Serves 6

- ½ cup unsalted butter, melted
- 1 cup granulated sugar
- 1 teaspoon dark rum
- 2 large eggs
- ½ cup all-purpose flour
- ⅓ cup unsweetened cocoa powder
- ¼ teaspoon baking powder
- Pinch of kosher salt

1. Preheat the Ninja Foodi 2-Basket Air Fryer to 350°F.
2. In a large mixing bowl, whisk together melted butter, eggs, and dark rum until light and fluffy.
3. In a separate bowl, combine flour, sugar, cocoa powder, salt, and baking powder.
4. Gradually add the dry ingredients to the wet ingredients, stirring continuously until the batter is smooth and free of lumps.
5. Grease two air fryer-safe cake pans and divide the batter evenly between them.
6. Place one pan in each of the two air fryer baskets.
7. Bake for 20-25 minutes, or until a toothpick inserted into the center comes out clean.
8. Allow the brownies to cool in the pans for 10 minutes before cutting and serving.

CHEESECAKE CUPS

Prep time: 5 minutes | **Cook time:** 10 minutes | **Serves** 6

- 8 ounces cream cheese, softened
- ¼ cup plain whole-milk Greek yogurt
- 1 large egg
- 1 teaspoon pure vanilla extract
- 3 tablespoons monk fruit sweetener
- ¼ teaspoon kosher salt
- ½ cup walnuts, roughly chopped

1. Preheat the Ninja Foodi 2-Basket Air Fryer to 315°F.
2. In a large mixing bowl, use a hand mixer to beat together cream cheese, yogurt, egg, vanilla extract, sweetener, and salt until smooth and well combined.
3. Gently fold in the chopped walnuts.
4. Place 6 silicone muffin liners in two air fryer-safe pans (this makes removal easier).
5. Divide the cheesecake batter evenly among the muffin liners, placing 3 muffin liners in each pan.
6. Place one pan in each air fryer basket.
7. Cook for 10 minutes, or until the tops are lightly browned and the cheesecake cups are set.
8. Remove from the air fryer and refrigerate for 3 hours to firm up before serving.

CHOCOLATE CHIP MUFFINS

Prep time: 12 minutes | **Cook time:** 15 minutes | **Serves** 2

- Pinch of kosher salt
- 2 large eggs
- ⅓ cup light brown sugar
- ⅓ cup unsalted butter, softened
- 4 tablespoons whole milk
- ¼ teaspoon vanilla extract
- ½ teaspoon baking powder
- 1 cup all-purpose flour
- 1 pouch chocolate chips

1. Prepare 4 oven-safe ramekins by lining them with muffin papers.
2. In a large bowl, use an electric mixer to beat eggs, brown sugar, butter, milk, and vanilla extract until well combined.
3. In a separate bowl, whisk together flour, baking powder, and salt.
4. Gradually add dry ingredients to wet ingredients, mixing until just combined.
5. Gently fold in chocolate chips, ensuring even distribution.
6. Divide batter evenly among the 4 ramekins.
7. Place ramekins in both air fryer baskets.
8. Set Zone 1 basket to Air Fry mode at 350°F for 15 minutes.
9. Press the MATCH button to apply the same settings to Zone 2 basket.
10. If muffins are not fully cooked after 15 minutes, air fry for an additional 1-2 minutes.

AIR FRYER SWEET TWISTS

Prep time: 15 minutes | **Cook time:** 9 minutes | **Serves** 2

- 1 sheet store-bought puff pastry, thawed
- ½ teaspoon ground cinnamon
- ½ teaspoon granulated sugar
- ½ teaspoon black sesame seeds
- Pinch of kosher salt
- 2 tablespoons freshly grated Parmesan cheese

1. Place thawed puff pastry on a clean work surface.
2. In a small bowl, mix Parmesan cheese, sugar, salt, sesame seeds, and cinnamon.
3. Press the spice mixture onto both sides of the pastry.
4. Cut the pastry into 1 x 3-inch strips.
5. Twist each strip twice from both ends.
6. Transfer twists to both air fryer baskets.
7. Set Zone 1 basket to Air Fry mode at 400°F for 9-10 minutes.
8. Press the MATCH button to apply the same settings to Zone 2 basket.
9. Serve immediately after cooking.

JELLY DONUTS

Prep time: 5 minutes | **Cook time:** 25 minutes | **Serves** 4

- 1 package Pillsbury Grands Homestyle Biscuits
- ½ cup seedless raspberry jelly
- 1 tablespoon unsalted butter, melted
- ½ cup granulated sugar

1. Install crisper plates in both air fryer drawers.
2. Divide biscuits evenly between Zone 1 basket and Zone 2 basket baskets.
3. Set Zone 1 basket to Air Fry mode at 390°F for 22 minutes.
4. Press the MATCH button to apply the same settings to Zone 2 basket.
5. Place sugar in a wide, shallow bowl.
6. Once biscuits are cooked, brush all sides with melted butter.
7. Roll buttered biscuits in sugar to coat completely.
8. Using a long cake decorating tip, pipe 1-2 tablespoons of raspberry jelly into each biscuit.

CHOCOLATE CAKE

Prep time: 5 minutes | **Cook time:** 20 minutes | **Serves** 8

- ½ cup granulated sugar
- ¼ cup plus 3 tablespoons all-purpose flour
- 3 tablespoons unsweetened cocoa powder
- ½ teaspoon baking powder
- ½ teaspoon baking soda
- ¼ teaspoon kosher salt
- 1 large egg
- 2 tablespoons vegetable oil
- ½ cup whole milk
- ½ teaspoon vanilla extract

1. Preheat the Ninja Foodi 2-Basket Air Fryer to 330°F.
2. Grease and flour two 6 x 6-inch baking pans (one for each basket).
3. In a medium bowl, whisk together sugar, flour, cocoa powder, baking powder, baking soda, and salt.
4. Add the egg, vegetable oil, milk, and vanilla extract, and whisk until smooth and well combined.
5. Divide the batter evenly between the two prepared pans.
6. Place one pan in each air fryer basket and bake for 20 minutes, or until a toothpick inserted in the centre comes out clean or with just a few crumbs.
7. Once done, allow the cakes to cool slightly before serving.

AIR FRIED BANANAS

Prep time: 10 minutes | **Cook time:** 13 minutes | **Serves** 4

- 4 ripe bananas, sliced
- Avocado oil cooking spray

1. Spread banana slices in a single layer on the crisper plates.
2. Lightly spray banana slices with avocado oil.
3. Place crisper plates in the Ninja Foodi 2-Basket Air Fryer.
4. Set Zone 1 basket to Air Fry mode at 350°F for 13 minutes.
5. Press the MATCH button to apply the same settings to Zone 2 basket.
6. Press START to begin cooking.
7. Serve warm.

APPLE NUTMEG FLAUTAS

Prep time: 10 minutes | Cook time: 8 minutes | Serves 8

- ¼ cup light brown sugar
- ⅛ cup all-purpose flour
- ¼ teaspoon ground cinnamon
- Freshly grated nutmeg, to taste
- 4 apples, peeled, cored, and sliced
- ½ lemon, juiced
- 6 (10-inch) flour tortillas
- Vegetable oil spray
- Caramel sauce (for serving)
- Cinnamon sugar (for garnish)

1. In a large bowl, mix brown sugar, cinnamon, nutmeg, and flour.
2. Toss apple slices with lemon juice, then add to the sugar mixture and mix well.
3. Lay out a tortilla and add ½ cup of the apple mixture.
4. Roll the tortilla into a tight burrito, securing with a toothpick.
5. Repeat with remaining tortillas and apple mixture.
6. Place two apple burritos on each crisper plate and lightly spray with cooking oil.
7. Set Zone 1 basket to Air Fry mode at 400°F for 8 minutes.
8. Press the MATCH button to apply the same settings to Zone 2 basket.
9. Halfway through cooking, flip the burritos.
10. Garnish with caramel sauce and cinnamon sugar before serving.

MEASUREMENT CONVERSION CHART

VOLUME EQUIVALENTS(DRY)

US STANDARD	METRIC (APPROXIMATE)
1/8 teaspoon	0.5 mL
1/4 teaspoon	1 mL
1/2 teaspoon	2 mL
3/4 teaspoon	4 mL
1 teaspoon	5 mL
1 tablespoon	15 mL
1/4 cup	59 mL
1/2 cup	118 mL
3/4 cup	177 mL
1 cup	235 mL
2 cups	475 mL
3 cups	700 mL
4 cups	1 L

VOLUME EQUIVALENTS(LIQUID)

US STANDARD	US STANDARD (OUNCES)	METRIC (APPROXIMATE)
2 tablespoons	1 fl.oz.	30 mL
1/4 cup	2 fl.oz.	60 mL
1/2 cup	4 fl.oz.	120 mL
1 cup	8 fl.oz.	240 mL
1 1/2 cup	12 fl.oz.	355 mL
2 cups or 1 pint	16 fl.oz.	475 mL
4 cups or 1 quart	32 fl.oz.	1 L
1 gallon	128 fl.oz.	4 L

TEMPERATURES EQUIVALENTS

FAHRENHEIT(F)	CELSIUS(C) (APPROXIMATE)
225 °F	107 °C
250 °F	120 °C
275 °F	135 °C
300 °F	150 °C
325 °F	160 °C
350 °F	180 °C
375 °F	190 °C
400 °F	205 °C
425 °F	220 °C
450 °F	235 °C
475 °F	245 °C
500 °F	260 °C

WEIGHT EQUIVALENTS

US STANDARD	METRIC (APPROXIMATE)
1 ounce	28 g
2 ounces	57 g
5 ounces	142 g
10 ounces	284 g
15 ounces	425 g
16 ounces (1 pound)	455 g
1.5 pounds	680 g
2 pounds	907 g

The Dirty Dozen and Clean Fifteen

The Environmental Working Group (EWG) is a nonprofit, nonpartisan organization dedicated to protecting human health and the environment Its mission is to empower people to live healthier lives in a healthier environment. This organization publishes an annual list of the twelve kinds of produce, in sequence, that have the highest amount of pesticide residue-the Dirty Dozen-as well as a list of the fifteen kinds ofproduce that have the least amount of pesticide residue-the Clean Fifteen.

THE DIRTY DOZEN

- The 2016 Dirty Dozen includes the following produce. These are considered among the year's most important produce to buy organic:

Strawberries	Spinach
Apples	Tomatoes
Nectarines	Bell peppers
Peaches	Cherry tomatoes
Celery	Cucumbers
Grapes	Kale/collard greens
Cherries	Hot peppers

- *The Dirty Dozen list contains two additional itemskale/collard greens and hot peppers-because they tend to contain trace levels of highly hazardous pesticides.*

THE CLEAN FIFTEEN

- The least critical to buy organically are the Clean Fifteen list. The following are on the 2016 list:

Avocados	Papayas
Corn	Kiw
Pineapples	Eggplant
Cabbage	Honeydew
Sweet peas	Grapefruit
Onions	Cantaloupe
Asparagus	Cauliflower
Mangos	

- *Some of the sweet corn sold in the United States are made from genetically engineered (GE) seedstock. Buy organic varieties of these crops to avoid GE produce.*

APPENDIX 3: INDEX

Hey there!

Wow, can you believe we've reached the end of this culinary journey together? I'm truly thrilled and filled with joy as I think back on all the recipes we've shared and the flavors we've discovered. This experience, blending a bit of tradition with our own unique twists, has been a journey of love for good food. And knowing you've been out there, giving these dishes a try, has made this adventure incredibly special to me.

Even though we're turning the last page of this book, I hope our conversation about all things delicious doesn't have to end. I cherish your thoughts, your experiments, and yes, even those moments when things didn't go as planned. Every piece of feedback you share is invaluable, helping to enrich this experience for us all.

I'd be so grateful if you could take a moment to share your thoughts with me, be it through a review on Amazon or any other place you feel comfortable expressing yourself online. Whether it's praise, constructive criticism, or even an idea for how we might do things differently in the future, your input is what truly makes this journey meaningful.

This book is a piece of my heart, offered to you with all the love and enthusiasm I have for cooking. But it's your engagement and your words that elevate it to something truly extraordinary.

Thank you from the bottom of my heart for being such an integral part of this culinary adventure. Your openness to trying new things and sharing your experiences has been the greatest gift.

Catch you later,

Betty J. Lawson

Printed in Great Britain
by Amazon

58641537R00044